Meteorology
The Study of Weather

CHRISTINE TAYLOR-BUTLER

Children's Press®
An Imprint of Scholastic Inc.
New York Toronto London Auckland Sydney
Mexico City New Delhi Hong Kong
Danbury, Connecticut

Content Consultant

Jack Williams

Founding editor of the *USA Today* weather pages and author of
THE AMS Weather Book: The Ultimate Guide to America's Weather

Library of Congress Cataloging-in-Publication Data

Taylor-Butler, Christine.
  Meteorology the study of weather/by Christine Taylor-Butler.
     p. cm.—(A true book)
  Includes bibliographical references and index.
  ISBN-13: 978-0-531-24678-8 (lib. bdg.)   ISBN-10: 0-531-24678-7 (lib. bdg.)
  ISBN-13: 978-0-531-28272-4 (pbk.)   ISBN-10: 0-531-28272-4 (pbk.)
  1. Meteorology—Juvenile literature. I. Title. II. Series.
  QC863.5.T39 2012
  551.5—dc23   2011030964

All rights reserved. Published in 2012 by Children's Press, an imprint of Scholastic Inc.
Printed in the United States of America
SCHOLASTIC, CHILDREN'S PRESS, A TRUE BOOK, and associated logos are trademarks and/or registered trademarks of Scholastic Inc.
5 6 7 8 9 10 R 21 20 19 18 17 16

Find the Truth!

Everything you are about to read is true *except* for one of the sentences on this page.

Which one is **TRUE**?

T or F   Jet streams are currents of air created by airplanes.

T or F   Water movement in the atmosphere may cause lightning.

Find the answers in this book.

Contents

THE BIG TRUTH!

Aristotle

Meteorologists work hard to keep track of the weather.

The first U.S. telegraph line was built in 1844.

Meteorologists let
you know when to
expect rain.

CHAPTER 1

Rain or Shine?

You check the weather report before you go to school. The weather service issues a thunderstorm watch for noon. But it's sunny outside now. There are no clouds in the sky. You take an umbrella just in case. Suddenly, the sky turns dark, and a storm appears. How does the weather service know about something that will happen in the future? The men and women who work there use a science called meteorology.

← Seventy-eight percent of all rain occurs over oceans.

The Study of Weather

Meteorology is the study of Earth's **atmosphere**. It comes from the Greek word *meteoron*, which means studying things high in the sky. The atmosphere is the layer of gases above Earth's surface. Scientists study the atmosphere to predict the weather. They also use this information to determine how Earth's climate is changing. Scientists who study the atmosphere are called meteorologists.

Meteorologists use science to forecast the weather.

8

Modern equipment can see weather before it moves into your area.

Meteorologists use radar, satellites, thermometers, and other devices to track the current weather. They also use ocean buoys, weather balloons, and reports from airline pilots. They use this information to forecast what the weather is likely to do in the next few hours and days. These forecasts help weather service meteorologists know when to issue storm and flood warnings. The warnings help people prepare for an emergency.

Climate change can lead to an increase in extreme weather such as hurricanes.

Studying the weather helps meteorologists predict climate changes around the world. Climate change can lead to drought that harms crops and wildlife. A drought can result in dust storms or forest fires. Global warming is causing glaciers to melt. This raises the ocean levels and causes flooding in coastal areas. Climate change impacts the environment and can affect human health by reducing air quality, increasing the occurrence of extreme weather, and damaging food supplies.

Businesses depend on accurate weather forecasts to plan their schedules. The forecasts help airline pilots and ship's captains avoid storms. Forecasts help farmers know when to plant and harvest crops. Cities use forecasts to prepare for floods and plan for snow removal. Ski resorts use forecasts to determine if there will be enough snow on a mountain for ski season. Schools use these same forecasts to decide if they need to close.

Towns and cities must prepare for snow storms ahead of time to make sure roads stay clear.

Storms were a major threat to the wooden ships that people used centuries ago.

CHAPTER 2

Meteorology in History

In early civilizations, sailors tried to predict the weather to plan safe routes across the oceans. In 3,000 BCE, people in India studied the skies and kept records of cloud formations. Ancient Egyptians planned their lives around seasonal flooding on the Nile. Ancient China kept records of weather patterns. For many people, understanding weather meant the difference between life and death.

← Ancient sailors believed that dumping petroleum oil into the sea would calm a storm.

Early Meteorologists

Early scientists observed the moon, sun, and stars to predict weather. Some studied animal behavior. Greek writer Theophrastus used these incorrect methods to write about weather in the 300s BCE. Other theories were more accurate. In 350 BCE, Greek philosopher Aristotle wrote that water **evaporated** from the oceans and other bodies of

water and returned as rain.

It was centuries before meteorologists invented the right tools to measure and predict weather accurately. This helped meteorologists understand which early theories were true.

Aristotle made many important scientific discoveries.

The invention of the barometer was an important step toward more accurate weather forecasts.

An Important Discovery

In 1643 and 1644, Italian mathematician Evangelista Torricelli filled glass tubes with mercury. He then turned them upside down and put them into an open container of mercury. The height of the mercury in the tube changed during the day. Torricelli realized that the mercury was responding to pressure changes in the atmosphere. When the mercury dropped, a storm approached. This observation led to the invention of the **barometer**.

Today, many thermometers measure the temperature in both Fahrenheit and Celsius.

To measure temperature, scientists experimented with a **thermoscope**. Temperature was estimated according to the height of water in a glass tube. But it was not accurate. In 1714, Daniel Fahrenheit began working with thermometers using mercury-filled tubes. In 1724, he created a scale that set 32 degrees as the freezing point of water and 212 degrees as the boiling point. In 1742, Anders Celsius developed a scale that eventually used zero for the freezing point and 100 as the boiling point.

In 1792, *The Old Farmer's Almanac* was created to provide farmers with weather forecasts, planting charts, and astronomy information. The publisher, Robert Thomas, studied solar activity, weather patterns, and the stars. He used a secret formula for creating his forecasts. The "secret" is kept in a black tin box in Dublin, New Hampshire. The almanac is still in use today, though its weather forecasts are not very accurate. Modern meteorology methods have replaced the almanac for many people.

Only the almanac's editors are allowed to see Thomas's secret formula for forecasting.

The Farmer's Almanac has been helping farmers predict the weather for hundreds of years.

Disaster Leads to Solutions

In 1854, 39 British and French military ships sank in a storm near Ukraine. Although meteorologists had tracked the storm as it moved across Europe, there was no way to warn the ships of the approaching danger. To avoid another disaster, France developed an early warning system and the first weather maps in 1863. They used the newly invented telegraph to send the information.

The telegraph changed the way people communicated over long distances.

The National Weather Service

In 1849, the Smithsonian Institution sent weather
equipment to telegraph companies in the United States.
Data was collected from volunteers across the country.
By 1860, more than 500 stations were providing
weather information. The government needed a way to
analyze the information and create weather forecasts.
On February 9, 1870, President Ulysses S. Grant signed
a bill creating the Weather Bureau. In 1970, it was
renamed the National Weather Service.

★ TORNADO!

A tornado is a rotating column of air. Its wind has enough energy to destroy a city. A tornado can travel up to 70 miles (112.7 kilometers) per hour. Its rotating wind speeds can reach greater than 200 miles per hour (321.9 kph).

Tornadoes start with a thunderstorm. The strongest storms are called supercells. A supercell can be as wide as 10 miles (16.1 km) in diameter and as high as 50,000 feet (15,240 meters).

In the United States, hot, dry air from the Rocky Mountains in the west meets warm, moist air from the east. The rising air begins to rotate.

Tornadoes are visible because they are filled with water drops, dust, and debris.

Waterspouts are tornadoes that form over water.

Some climates have heavy
snowfall in the winter months.

CHAPTER 3

What Is Weather?

Some people believe that weather and climate mean the same thing. Actually, they do not. Climate is the average weather of an environment over hundreds of years. For example, some places have dry desert climates. Other places have moist tropical climates. Weather is something that happens in the atmosphere at a specific time. Rain, snow, and wind are types of weather.

In 1884, scientist Wladimir Köppen divided Earth into five major zones: tropical, dry, temperate, cold, and polar.

Changes in the Troposphere

Weather takes place in the lower layer of the atmosphere, where we live. This area is called the **troposphere**. The troposphere can be as high as 12 miles (19.3 km) at the equator and 4 miles (6.4 km) at each pole. The atmosphere acts like a layer of insulation around the planet. It traps the sun's heat and warms the earth. Without it, Earth would enter an ice age.

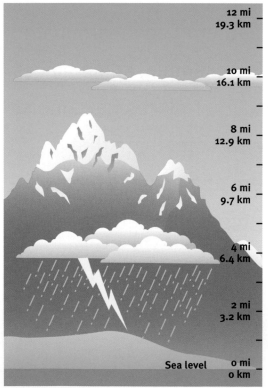

12 mi
19.3 km

10 mi
16.1 km

8 mi
12.9 km

6 mi
9.7 km

4 mi
6.4 km

2 mi
3.2 km

Sea level   0 mi
0 km

The temperature is colder at the top of the troposphere than at the bottom.

Clouds and weather all occur in the troposphere.

Half of all air molecules are in the first 18,000 feet (5,486.4 m) of the troposphere.

People are often caught outside during unexpected weather changes.

Weather changes quickly. When the sun heats the earth, air molecules near the surface move farther apart. The warm air rises. Winds blow across the ground, bringing in cooler air to replace it. Winds will blow as long as air is rising. At the same time, air in other places cools and sinks. It then feeds the winds, which bring it into areas with rising air.

Large storm fronts can sometimes be seen from miles away.

The boundary between cold air and warm air is called a **weather front**. Meteorologists often use this term when giving a forecast. Cold fronts usually move from northwest to southeast in North America. They carry heavy, colder air. Warm fronts generally move from southwest to northeast. They carry lighter, warmer air.

Thunderstorms are sometimes created when the heavy, colder air pushes beneath lighter, warmer air. If the temperature difference is large, severe storms may form.

Jet Streams

Jet streams are fast-moving wind currents found in the upper part of the troposphere. They are common in the winter when the temperature difference is greatest between warm air from the equator and cold arctic air. Jet streams' high winds can cause problems for aircraft flying at high altitudes. Meteorologists alert these aircraft when they might be in danger of the turbulence caused by jet streams.

Jet stream clouds can sometimes be seen from outer space.

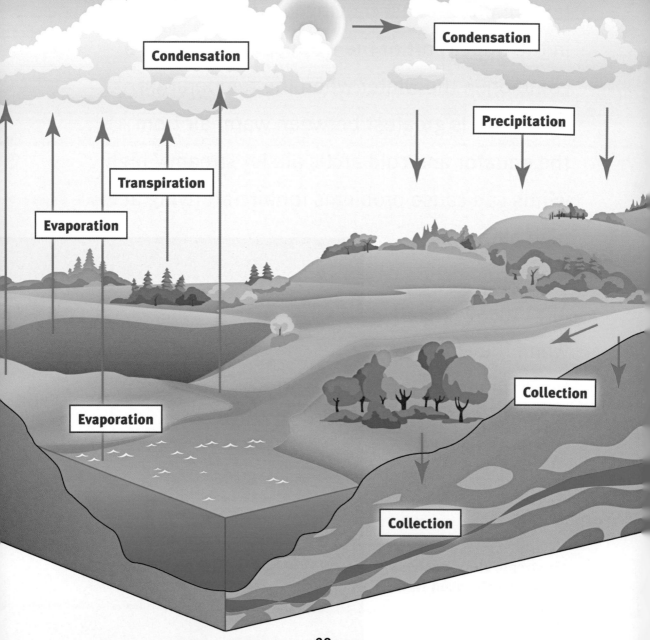

The water cycle connects all of the water on Earth.

Condensation

Condensation

Precipitation

Transpiration

Evaporation

Evaporation

Collection

Collection

CHAPTER 4

The "Weather Engine"

Water is always moving from Earth's surface to the atmosphere and back again. This is called the hydrologic cycle. Another name for this is the water cycle. This cycle relates to weather patterns and climate. Solar energy warms water on Earth's surface and causes it to evaporate. Plants also lose water through a process called **transpiration**. Transpiration is similar to how humans lose water when they sweat.

← The amount of water on Earth is the same as when the planet formed.

Precipitation

When water vapor rises into the air, the vapor cools. This causes it to **condense** and form clouds. Some of the vapor becomes liquid and falls back to the surface as rain, sleet, or snow. This action is called **precipitation**. Wind currents can carry water vapor to other areas before it returns to Earth's surface.

Each raindrop contains 1.7 sextillion molecules. That's 17 followed by 20 zeroes!

Sleet forms when raindrops or melted snowflakes freeze.

Hurricanes

Most of Earth's water is stored in oceans. The oceans absorb energy from the sun and release it slowly into the atmosphere. Warm ocean waters provide fuel for severe storms in late

The center, or eye, of a hurricane is always calm.

summer months. Storms and wind sometimes begin to spiral counterclockwise. They enter an area of low pressure, gaining water and energy. These storms are called hurricanes when their wind speeds reach 75 miles per hour (120.7 kph).

Some hurricanes can travel long distances. In 2011, Hurricane Irene caused severe damage as far north as New Hampshire.

Lightning can strike the earth 50 miles (80.4 km) from a storm cloud.

Lightning and Thunder

Water movement may also contribute to lightning. A strong draft of air can move water drops up as high as 70,000 feet (21,336 m) in the atmosphere. The water freezes quickly. When a downdraft pushes the drops lower, the drops' surfaces melt. When the frozen and melted water collide, electrons break off. This creates a negative charge at the base of the cloud and a positive one at the top. When enough charge builds up, lightning results.

Lightning releases an enormous amount of heat in a fraction of a second—almost 54,000 degrees Fahrenheit (30,000 degrees Celsius). This causes the air to expand rapidly. When this happens, the energy released creates an explosive shock wave a person can hear. We call the sound thunder. Because lightning can strike far from a storm, meteorologists warn people to stay indoors for at least 30 minutes after the last clap of thunder to avoid being struck.

Lightning is a powerful form of static electricity.

Meteorologists get information from weather stations all around the world.

CHAPTER 5

Meteorology in Action

The National Weather Service is part of the National Oceanic and Atmospheric Administration (NOAA). NOAA uses advanced technology to collect data from space, the air, the oceans, and the ground. Supercomputers in Washington, D.C., convert the data into weather forecasts and send it to weather offices throughout the country. The information you see on television or hear on the radio comes from these sources.

Weather Satellites

Satellites transmit images of weather from space. NOAA uses two types of satellites. One orbits 540 miles (869 km) above Earth. The other orbits at more than 22,000 miles (35,406 km). These satellites can monitor floods, dust storms, fires, snow, volcanic activity, and other events on Earth's surface.

Satellites also study solar radiation and flares. These forms of energy can enter the atmosphere and cause changes in Earth's weather or radio blackouts.

Timeline of Weather Prediction

1814
The first U.S. weather observation stations are created at army posts.

1842
Christian Doppler discovers an effect that becomes known as the Doppler effect.

1870
Congress creates the Weather Bureau, controlled by the secretary of war.

Weather Balloons

The weather service releases more than 100 helium or hydrogen balloons each day. Transmitters called **radiosondes** are attached to the balloons. Radiosondes send temperature, pressure, and humidity data to ground stations. Tracking the balloon allows wind direction and speed to be measured. When the balloon bursts, a parachute opens, allowing the radiosonde to drop safely to the ground.

1926
The Weather Bureau begins providing forecasts to aircraft outside of the military.

1909
The United States begins using balloons to monitor weather in the atmosphere.

1960
NASA launches the first weather satellite, called TIROS-1.

Doppler Radar

Meteorologists often refer to "Doppler radar" during a weather forecast. This radar system sends out a burst of microwave energy. When the wave bounces off an object, part of the wave returns to the radar. The change in shape, position, and **frequency** of the wave shows the location, speed, and type of weather it bounced off of. The shift in frequency is known as the Doppler effect. Doppler radar sends and "listens" to energy waves 1,300 times each second.

There are Doppler radar systems all around the world.

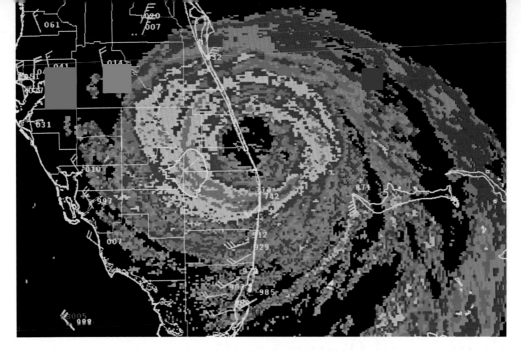

Yellow and red colors show where a storm is strongest on a Doppler image.

Math formulas are used to convert the data into images and timetables. These images are then combined with maps of the country. This allows viewers to "see" the weather in the area during television broadcasts. The weather service also broadcasts weather reports on certain radio frequencies. You can buy a weather radio at the store. Your car radio may be equipped with a weather band.

Buoys are located far from land.

Buoys and Ocean Spotters

Weather buoys are located in oceans around the world. The buoys record wind direction, barometric pressure, water temperature, humidity, and wave height. Each buoy has its own identification number. Ships can use the number to access the buoy's records and learn about the weather in the area.

NOAA also collects weather information from volunteers traveling on more than 1,000 ships at sea. This information can be more accurate than satellite data during severe storms.

Flying Into the Eye of a Storm

To help meteorologists with their research, the Air Force Reserve's 53rd Weather Reconnaissance Squadron flies directly into violent storms. It enters the storms at 10,000 feet (3,048 m). Weather data is sent directly from special military planes to the National Weather Service. There are 10 full-time crews and 10 part-time crews. Some crew members are also teachers, commercial pilots, or computer specialists. The squadron sometimes fly into three storms each day.

So You Want to Be a Meteorologist?

Meteorologists work in a wide variety of fields. They are scientists, engineers, teachers, and journalists who love weather. The person you see on television is only part of the team that brings weather reports to you. Many work in offices analyzing computer data. Others go to the location to investigate. Meteorologists study math, science, geography, and computer science in college before receiving a degree. The job also requires strong communication skills. It just might be the right job for you someday! ★

A team of meteorologists launch a weather balloon to gather data.

True Statistics

Coldest temperature measured on Earth:
Vostok Station, Antarctica, −128.6°F
(−89.2°C)

Hottest temperature measured on Earth: El
Azizia, Libya, 136° F (57.8°C)

**Average number of tornadoes that occur in the
United States:** 1,000 each year

**Greatest number of tornadoes to occur in one
day:** More than 300 in April 2011

**Greatest amount of annual snowfall in the
United States:** 1,140 ft. (347.5 m) on Mount
Baker in Washington State, 1998–1999

City with the highest average annual rainfall:
Lloro, Colombia, at 523.6 in. (1,330 cm)

Did you find the truth?

F Jet streams are currents of air
created by airplanes.

T Water movement in the
atmosphere may cause lightning.

Resources

Books

Chambers, Catherine. *Hurricanes*. New York: Children's Press, 2005.

Fleisher, Paul. *Doppler Radar, Satellites, and Computer Models: The Science of Weather Forecasting*. Minneapolis, MN: Lerner Books, 2010.

Fradin, Judy, and Dennis Fradin. *Tornado!* Washington, DC: National Geographic Children's Books, 2011.

Hanson, Anders. *Meteorologist's Tools*. Edina, MN: Super Sandcastle Books, 2011.

Sohn, Emily, and Erin Ash Sullivan. *Weather and the Water Cycle: Will It Rain?* Chicago: Norwood House Press, 2011.

Stiefel, Chana. *Forces of Nature*. New York: Scholastic, 2010.

Organizations and Web Sites

Hurricane Hunters Association
www.hurricanehunters.com/cyberflight.htm
Take a cyber flight with the crew into the eye of a hurricane.

National Weather Service Weather Forecast Office
www.crh.noaa.gov/cys/?n=officevirtualtour
Take an online tour of a Wyoming NOAA office in action.

Places to Visit

The Dave Fultz Memorial Laboratory for Hydrodynamics
University of Chicago
Henry Hinds Laboratory
5734 South Ellis Avenue
Chicago, IL 60637
(773) 702-1234
http://geosci.uchicago.edu/~nnn/LAB

National Weather Service: Raleigh Forecast Office
1005 Capability Drive
Suite 300
Centennial Campus
Raleigh, NC 27606-5226
(919) 515-8209
www.erh.noaa.gov/rah/tours

 Visit this Scholastic web site for more information on meteorology:
www.factsfornow.scholastic.com

Important Words

atmosphere (AT-muhs-feer) – the mixture of gases that surrounds a planet

barometer (buh-RAH-mi-tur) – an instrument that measures changes in air pressure and is used to forecast the weather

condense (kuhn-DENS) – to turn from a gas into a liquid, usually as a result of cooling

evaporated (ee-VAP-uh-rate-id) – changed into a vapor or gas

frequency (FREE-kwuhn-see) – the number of cycles, or waves, per second of a radio wave

precipitation (pri-sip-i-TAY-shuhn) – the falling of water from the sky in the form of rain, sleet, or snow

radiosondes (RAY-dee-oh-sahndz) – radio transmitters attached to weather balloons

thermoscope (THER-muh-skope) – an early tool used to measure temperature by using water

transpiration (tran-spuh-RAY-shuhn) – the process by which plants give off moisture

troposphere (TROH-pus-feer) – the layer of atmosphere closest to Earth's surface

weather front (WETH-ur FRUHNT) – the boundary between cold polar air and warm tropical air

Index

Page numbers in **bold** indicate illustrations

About the Author

Christine Taylor-Butler is the author of more than 60 books for children, including the True Book series on American History/Government, Health and the Human Body, and Science Experiments. A graduate of Massachusetts Institute of Technology, Christine holds degrees in both civil engineering and art and design. She currently lives in Kansas City, Missouri.